Anne Wils

*Classic*
*Essential*

# Casseroles

**KÖNEMANN**

# ~Creating Casseroles~

Casseroles are delicious, nutritious, and simple to make. By slowly cooking the meat and vegetables with the stock and meat juices, a rich sauce develops, rewarding you with a well-balanced and flavoursome meal.

## Cooking equipment
Before you start thinking about *what* to cook, you should decide what you are going to cook it *in*. For starters, it is worth investing in a good-quality casserole in a size that suits your lifestyle (it really is a case of getting what you pay for). There are two types of casserole available—flameproof and ovenproof. They both have a tight-fitting lid to ensure that no steam escapes and the condensation falls back into the casserole while cooking. The result? A moist and tender dish with all the flavours well combined.

### *Flameproof casseroles*
Usually made of cast iron or enamelled cast iron, these casseroles retain their heat, so you should remove your meal once it is cooked, or it will continue to cook. These casseroles can be used on the stove top as well as in the oven, giving you the convenience of cooking and serving your meal in one dish.

### *Ovenproof casseroles*
Because some ceramic casseroles can't be used on the stove top, always check the manufacturer's instructions before use. If your casserole is unsuitable for the stove top, seal or brown the ingredients in a heavy-based pan before transferring to the casserole. Pour in a little stock or water and gently scrape the pan juices into the casserole.

## Choosing the meat
Less expensive cuts of meat are perfect for casseroling as the slow-cooking process tenderises the meat. Use well-marbled beef, and don't be put off by exterior fat as this can easily be trimmed. Leave the marbled fat and any sinew as it will dissolve and gelatinise during lengthy cooking, resulting in meat that melts in your mouth and a rich and tasty sauce.

## Coating and browning
Coating the meat with flour helps to brown and thicken the sauce during cooking, so that you don't have to thicken it at the end. Put the flour in a plastic bag, add the meat in batches, seal and give it a good shake. Shake off any excess flour.

*It is important to know whether your casserole is flame-proof (on the left) or ovenproof (on the right).*

## Cuts of meat suitable for casseroling

*Beef* blade, brisket, chuck, gravy, round, shank, silver-side, skirt, spare ribs, topside

*Veal* knuckle (osso buco), leg, shoulder

*Lamb* best neck and forequarter chops, neck rosette, shank, diced forequarter, boneless shoulder

*Pork* forequarter or loin chops, neck, fillets, diced shoulder, medallions

*Chicken* thigh fillets or cutlets, pieces

To brown the meat, heat some oil and butter in a pan and cook the coated meat over high heat in batches to add flavour and colour. Don't overcrowd the pan, otherwise the meat will stew in its juices and toughen.

## Cooking tips
Always simmer (never boil) the meat to prevent it from toughening.

Add any vegetables you wish to remain whole half an hour before the end of cooking.

Use a fork to test if the meat is cooked. If it falls easily from the fork and the sauce is thick, it's ready. If the meat clings to the fork and the sauce is thin, continue cooking for a little while longer.

If the sauce is still thin when the meat is cooked, uncover the casserole, remove the meat and cook the sauce over medium heat on the stove top until it reduces and thickens.

## Reheating from the fridge
The beauty of a casserole is that you can make it up to 2 days in advance. In fact, it tastes much better if you do! Store in the refrigerator until you need it, then transfer to a large pan or flameproof casserole. Bring to the boil, then reduce the heat and simmer until piping hot all the way though.

## Reheating from the freezer
Most casseroles can be frozen for up to 1 month (with the exception of seafood casseroles). When the casserole has cooled, skim off any solidified fat and transfer to an airtight container and cover with plastic wrap to prevent freezer burn, or double bag in freezer bags. A useful tip is to freeze in portion sizes to suit the number of people you are likely to cook for. Always thaw the casserole completely in the fridge overnight, then reheat as you would from the fridge.

Garlic should be added when reheating as freezing destroys the flavour. Don't add too much seasoning if you are freezing ahead as the flavour can intensify during freezing. Instead, season as you reheat.

## How to make a bouquet garni

Wrap the green part of a leek loosely around a couple of celery tops, a few stalks of fresh parsley, a sprig of fresh thyme and a bay leaf. Tie with kitchen string, leaving a long tail to the string for easy removal when you are ready to serve.

# ∼ Navarin of Lamb ∼

**Preparation time:**
20 minutes
**Total cooking time:**
2 hours 20 minutes
**Serves 4**

1.25 kg boned shoulder or leg of lamb (ask your butcher to bone the meat)
30 g butter
1 tablespoon oil
1 small onion, quartered
12 large bulb spring onions, stems removed
1 clove garlic, crushed
1 tablespoon plain flour
1 cup (250 ml) beef stock
1 turnip or swede, peeled and cubed
1 large carrot, thickly sliced
6 new potatoes, halved
400 g can chopped tomatoes
1 bouquet garni
1/2 cup (80 g) frozen peas

**1**∼Remove any excess fat from the lamb and cut the meat into bite-sized cubes. Preheat the oven to slow 150°C (300°F/Gas 2). Heat the butter and oil in a 2.5 litre flameproof casserole. Cook the onion and spring onions over medium heat for 5 minutes, or until the onion is soft. Add the garlic and cook for 1–2 minutes. Remove from the casserole.
**2**∼Add the lamb in batches to the casserole and brown quickly. When all the meat is browned return it all to the casserole with the onions and sprinkle with flour. Pour in the stock and cook, stirring, until the mixture is smooth and slightly thickened.
**3**∼Stir in the turnip or swede, carrot, potato, tomatoes and bouquet garni. Cover with a tight-fitting lid and bake for 2 hours, or until the lamb is tender. Stir two to three times during cooking. Add the peas after 1 1/4 hours. Remove the bouquet garni before serving.

NUTRITION PER SERVE
Protein 75 g; Fat 18 g; Carbohydrate 13 g; Dietary Fibre 5 g; Cholesterol 225 mg; 2175 kJ (520 cal)

**Storage time**∼This casserole will keep in an airtight container in the refrigerator for up to 3 days. Reheat at moderate 180°C (350°F/Gas 4) for 30 minutes, or until piping hot all the way through.
**Note**∼If preferred, lamb noisettes are also suitable for this recipe.

*Cook the onion and spring onions over medium heat until the onion is soft.*

*Return the meat and onions to the casserole, then add the flour and stock.*

# ～ Chicken Cacciatore ～

**Preparation time:**
45 minutes
**Total cooking time:**
1 hour 20 minutes
**Serves 4**

1.5 kg chicken pieces
20 g butter
1 tablespoon oil
20 g butter, extra
1 large onion, chopped
2 cloves garlic, chopped
1 small green capsicum,
   chopped
150 g mushrooms,
   thickly sliced
1 tablespoon plain flour

1 cup (250 ml) white wine
1 tablespoon white wine
   vinegar
4 tomatoes, peeled,
   seeded and chopped
2 tablespoons tomato
   paste
1/2 cup (90 g) small
   black olives
1/3 cup (20 g) chopped
   fresh parsley

1～Preheat the oven to moderate 180°C (350°F/Gas 4). Remove excess fat from the chicken and pat dry with paper towels. Heat half the butter and oil in a 2.5 litre flameproof casserole. Cook half the chicken over high heat until browned all over, then set aside. Heat the remaining butter and oil and cook the remaining chicken. Set aside.

2～Heat the extra butter in the casserole, and cook the onion and garlic for 2–3 minutes. Add the capsicum and mushrooms and cook, stirring, for 3 minutes more. Stir in the flour and cook for 1 minute. Add the wine, vinegar, tomato and tomato paste. Cook, stirring, for 2 minutes, or until slightly thickened.

3～Add the chicken to the casserole and make sure it is well coated in the tomato and onion mixture. Place in the oven and bake, covered, for 1 hour, or until the chicken is tender. Stir in the olives and parsley. Season well with salt and cracked pepper and serve with pasta.

**NUTRITION PER SERVE**
Protein 80 g; Fat 30 g; Carbohydrate 9 g; Dietary Fibre 4.5 g; Cholesterol 285 mg; 2810 kJ (670 cal)

**Note**～For a thicker sauce, remove the cooked chicken from the casserole dish and reduce the sauce over medium heat until thickened a little. Return the chicken to the casserole and add the olives and herbs. The French equivalent of this dish is Chicken Chasseur.

*Heat the butter and oil in the casserole and brown the chicken pieces in batches.*

*Add the flour to the capsicum and mushroom mixture.*

*Stir in the wine, vinegar, tomato and tomato paste, and cook until slightly thickened.*

*Add the chicken pieces, making sure they are well coated in the tomato mixture.*

# ∽ Beef Bourguignon ∽

**Preparation time:**
10 minutes
**Total cooking time:**
2 hours
**Serves 4–6**

| | |
|---|---|
| 1 kg topside or round steak | bouquet garni |
| 1/4 cup (30 g) plain flour | 1 cup (250 ml) red wine |
| 3 rashers bacon, rind removed | 2 cups (500 ml) beef stock |
| 1 tablespoon oil | 200 g button mushrooms |
| 12 pickling onions | 1 clove garlic, crushed |

**1** ∽ Trim the steak of fat and sinew, cut into cubes, and lightly coat in seasoned flour.
**2** ∽ Cut the bacon into squares. Heat the oil in a 2.5 litre flameproof casserole and quickly cook the bacon over medium heat. Remove. Brown the meat well in batches, remove and set aside, then add the onions and cook until browned.
**3** ∽ Return the meat and bacon to the casserole with the bouquet garni, wine, stock, mushrooms and garlic. Bring to the boil, then reduce the heat, cover and simmer for 1 1/2 hours, or until the meat is very tender, stirring occasionally. Remove the bouquet garni before serving.

**NUTRITION PER SERVE (6)**
Protein 40 g; Fat 10 g; Carbohydrate 7.5 g; Dietary Fibre 7 g; Cholesterol 90 mg; 1330 kJ (320 cal)

*Trim the steak, then cut into cubes with a sharp knife.*

*Cook the bacon quickly over medium heat, then remove from the casserole.*

*Add the pickling onions and cook, stirring, until well browned all over.*

*Return the bacon and meat to the casserole and add the bouquet garni.*

# ～ Veal Goulash ～

**Preparation time:**
35 minutes
**Total cooking time:**
2 hours
**Serves 4**

50 g butter
750 g veal shoulder,
  cut into 3 cm cubes
2 red onions, chopped
2 cloves garlic, chopped
1 tablespoon Hungarian
  paprika
1/4 teaspoon caraway
  seeds
4 tomatoes
1 sprig fresh marjoram

125 g button mushrooms
1 green capsicum,
  chopped
1 red capsicum,
  chopped
1 tablespoon tomato
  paste
sour cream, to serve
fresh marjoram leaves,
  to garnish

**1** ～ Preheat the oven to warm 160°C (315°F/ Gas 2–3). Heat the butter in a 2.5 litre flameproof casserole. Add the veal cubes and cook in batches, stirring, for 5 minutes, or until the meat has changed colour. Remove from the casserole. Cook the onion and garlic, stirring, for 5 minutes. Sprinkle on the paprika and caraway seeds. Stir to coat and cook for a further 5 minutes. Return the meat to the casserole.

**2** ～ Cut a small cross in the base of each tomato, place in a heatproof bowl and pour on boiling water. Leave for about 30 seconds, then remove the skins. Remove the seeds from the tomatoes with a teaspoon, then chop the flesh.

**3** ～ Add the marjoram sprig, mushrooms (halve any large mushrooms), green and red capsicum, tomato, tomato paste and 1/2 cup (125 ml) water to the veal. Stir thoroughly to combine. Cook, covered, in the oven for 1 3/4 hours, or until the veal is tender.

**4** ～ Remove the sprig of marjoram. Season well and serve with pasta or boiled potatoes and a dollop of sour cream. Garnish with marjoram leaves.

**NUTRITION PER SERVE**
Protein 45 g; Fat 15 g; Carbohydrate 8 g; Dietary Fibre 4 g; Cholesterol 190 mg; 1150 kJ (275 cal)

**Variation** ～ Use a 425 g can of whole peeled tomatoes, chopped, instead of the fresh tomatoes and leave out the 1/2 cup of water.

*Sprinkle the paprika and caraway seeds over the onion and garlic.*

*Leave the tomatoes in the boiling water for 30 seconds, then peel off the skins.*

*Use a teaspoon to remove the seeds from the tomatoes.*

*Add the remaining ingredients to the veal and stir thoroughly.*

# ~ Chickpea Casserole ~

**Preparation time:**
1 hour + overnight
soaking + 20 minutes
standing
**Total cooking time:**
1 hour 20 minutes
**Serves 6**

1 cup (220 g) dried
  chickpeas
1 small eggplant, cut
  into 2 cm cubes
2 tablespoons olive oil
2 onions, sliced
2 cloves garlic,
  crushed
2 tablespoons grated
  fresh ginger
1 tablespoon ground
  cumin
1–2 teaspoons chilli
  powder

2 teaspoons paprika
1.5 litres vegetable
  stock
2 carrots, thinly sliced
2 turnips, peeled and
  cut into 2 cm cubes
3 zucchini, cut into
  2 cm slices
300 g pumpkin, cut into
  3 cm cubes
2 tomatoes, chopped
1/3 cup (10 g) chopped
  flat-leaf parsley

1. Put the chickpeas in a bowl, cover with water and soak overnight. Rinse and drain.
2. Spread the eggplant out on a plate in a single layer and sprinkle generously with salt. Leave for 20 minutes, rinse well and pat dry with paper towels.
3. Heat the oil in a 2.5 litre flameproof casserole. Add the onion and cook over medium heat for 5 minutes, or until lightly golden, stirring occasionally. Add the garlic, ginger, cumin, chilli and paprika, and cook for 1 minute. Add the chickpeas to the casserole with the stock. Bring to the boil, then reduce the heat and simmer, covered, for 40 minutes, or until the chickpeas are just tender. Stir occasionally.
4. Add the carrot and turnip, and simmer for 15 minutes. Add the eggplant, zucchini, pumpkin and tomato, and simmer, covered, stirring occasionally, for 15 minutes, or until tender. Stir in the parsley and serve with rice.

**NUTRITION PER SERVE**
Protein 9 g; Fat 9 g;
Carbohydrate 20 g; Dietary
Fibre 9.5 g; Cholesterol 0 mg;
830 kJ (200 cal)

**Note.** This casserole can be made up to 2 days ahead and stored in an airtight container in the refrigerator.

*Soak the chickpeas overnight, then rinse and drain well.*

*Spread the eggplant out on a plate and sprinkle with plenty of salt.*

*Add the garlic, ginger and spices to the onion and stir-fry for 1 minute.*

*Add the eggplant, zucchini, pumpkin and tomato, and simmer until tender.*

# ~ Oxtail Ragout ~

**Preparation time:**
40 minutes +
3 hours soaking
**Total cooking time:**
4 hours
**Serves 4**

1 kg oxtail, cut into
  short pieces (ask your
  butcher to do this)
1/4 cup (30 g) plain flour
1 tablespoon oil
2 rashers bacon, rind
  removed, chopped
1 small onion, studded
  with 6 whole cloves

2 cloves garlic, crushed
2 carrots, quartered
  lengthways
1 1/2 cups (375 ml) beef
  or chicken stock
425 g can puréed tomato
1 parsnip, quartered
  lengthways
1 leek, thickly sliced

1 ~ Trim any excess fat from the oxtail, and place it in a large bowl. Cover with water and set aside for 3 hours. Drain well and transfer the meat to a 2.5 litre flameproof casserole. Cover with fresh water and bring to the boil. Reduce the heat and simmer for 10 minutes, regularly skimming any froth from the surface with a strainer or spoon. Drain the meat, allow to cool and pat dry with paper towels.

2 ~ Preheat the oven to slow 150°C (300°F/Gas 2). Coat the oxtail with seasoned flour, shaking off any excess. Heat the oil in the casserole, add the bacon and cook over medium heat for 3 minutes, stirring frequently, then remove.

3 ~ Add the oxtail to the casserole and cook over medium–high heat for 3 minutes, or until browned, stirring continuously.

4 ~ Add the bacon, onion, garlic and half the carrot. Stir in the combined stock and puréed tomato. Cover and bake in the oven for 3 hours. Add the remaining carrot, parsnip and leek, and cook for a further 30–40 minutes, or until the vegetables are tender. Remove the onion before serving.

**NUTRITION PER SERVE**
Protein 40 g; Fat 30 g; Carbohydrate 44 g; Dietary Fibre 12 g; Cholesterol 90 mg; 2885 kJ (720 cal)

**Note** ~ For best results, make this dish a day in advance and store in the refrigerator, then reheat at moderate 180°C (350°F/Gas 4) for 45 minutes, or until piping hot.

*Simmer the meat for 10 minutes, skimming any froth from the surface.*

*Add the floured oxtail and brown over medium heat.*

# ~ Normandy Pork ~

**Preparation time:**
30 minutes
**Total cooking time:**
1 hour
**Serves 4**

4 pork loin chops or
  medallions, about
  2.5 cm thick
1/4 cup (30 g) plain
  flour
1/2 teaspoon nutmeg
30 g butter
2 green apples, cored
  and each cut into
  8 slices
1 tablespoon oil
1 onion, finely chopped

1/4 cup (60 ml) cider
  vinegar
1 sprig fresh thyme
11/2 cups (375 ml) dry
  cider
20 g butter, extra
1/3 cup (80 ml) cream
1 tablespoon Calvados
  or brandy
fresh thyme sprigs,
  to garnish

1.~Preheat the oven to warm 160°C (315°F/ Gas 2–3). Trim the pork of rind and excess fat. Season 2 tablespoons flour with the nutmeg, salt and pepper, and lightly coat the pork. Shake off and reserve any excess flour.
2.~Heat the butter in a 2.5 litre flameproof casserole. Fry the apple in batches for 1 minute on each side, or until lightly browned. Remove. Add the oil to the butter and cook the pork for 2–3 minutes, or until evenly browned on both sides. Remove.
3.~Add the onion, vinegar and thyme to the casserole and boil for 2 minutes, or until reduced by half. Lower the heat; add the cider and cook for a further 2 minutes. Add the pork, coat well in the mixture, then bake, covered, for 30 minutes. Add the apple and cook for a further 15 minutes, or until the pork is tender.
4.~Arrange the pork and apple on a serving plate. Remove the thyme sprig and return the casserole to the stove top. Combine the extra butter and reserved flour in a bowl to form a paste. Gradually whisk knobs of the paste into the sauce, and bring slowly to the boil, whisking until thickened. Lower the heat and add the cream and Calvados. Spoon over the apple and pork. Garnish with thyme.

**NUTRITION PER SERVE**
Protein 30 g; Fat 25 g;
Carbohydrate 18 g; Dietary
Fibre 2 g; Cholesterol 113 mg;
1912 kJ (455 cal)

*Dip the pork in the seasoned flour and shake off any excess.*

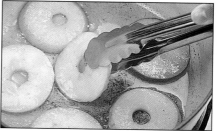

*Cook the apple rings in the butter until lightly browned on both sides.*

*Add the browned pork to the casserole and coat well in the mixture.*

*Gradually whisk small knobs of the butter and flour paste into the sauce.*

# ～ Chicken Gumbo ～

**Preparation time:**
35 minutes
**Total cooking time:**
1 hour 10 minutes
**Serves 4**

2 tablespoons vegetable oil
1 kg chicken pieces
3 rashers bacon, rind removed, roughly chopped
2–3 cloves garlic, crushed
6 spring onions, chopped into 4 cm lengths
1 green capsicum, seeded and chopped into 4 cm pieces
1 celery stick, roughly chopped
1 tablespoon plain flour
pinch cayenne pepper
1/4 teaspoon dried thyme leaves
1 bay leaf
1 cup (250 ml) chicken stock
425 g can chopped tomatoes
400 g small fresh okra
1/3 cup (20 g) chopped fresh parsley

1.～Heat half the oil in a 2.5 litre flameproof casserole. Pat the chicken pieces dry with paper towels, then add to the oil and brown over high heat for 2–3 minutes. Cook in two batches, then remove to a side plate.
2.～Heat the remaining oil in the casserole. Add the bacon, garlic and spring onion, and cook for 2–3 minutes. Add the capsicum and celery and cook, stirring, for 2–3 minutes. Sprinkle on the flour and cayenne pepper, then add the thyme and bay leaf. Cook, stirring, for a further 1 minute.

3.～Gradually stir in the chicken stock, bring to the boil and stir until thickened. Add the chopped tomatoes. Return the chicken to the casserole and stir to combine. Reduce the heat, cover and simmer for 30 minutes. Add the okra, stir through and cook for a further 20 minutes, or until the chicken is tender. Stir in the parsley and season to taste with salt and cracked black pepper. Serve over hot rice, spooning over the juices.

**NUTRITION PER SERVE**
Protein 65 g; Fat 15 g; Carbohydrate 9 g; Dietary Fibre 6.5 g; Cholesterol 140 mg; 1940 kJ (465 cal)

**Note**～Use an 825 g can of okra, drained, if fresh okra is not available.

*Brown the chicken pieces in batches over high heat.*

*Add the capsicum and celery to the bacon, garlic and spring onion mixture.*

*Sprinkle the flour over the bacon mixture, then add the cayenne pepper.*

*Add the okra to the gumbo and cook until the chicken is tender.*

# ~ Lancashire Hotpot ~

**Preparation time:**
40 minutes
**Total cooking time:**
2 hours
**Serves 8**

| | |
|---|---|
| 8 lamb forequarter chops, cut 2.5 cm thick | 2 large onions, sliced |
| 4 lamb kidneys, cut into quarters, cores removed | 1 large carrot, chopped |
| 1/4 cup (30 g) plain flour | 1 3/4 cups (440 ml) beef or vegetable stock |
| 50 g butter | 2 teaspoons chopped fresh thyme |
| 4 potatoes, thinly sliced | 1 bay leaf |
| | 30 g butter, melted |

1. ~Preheat the oven to warm 160°C (315°F/ Gas 2–3). Brush a 4 litre ovenproof casserole with melted butter or oil. Trim the meat of excess fat and sinew. Coat the chops and kidneys with seasoned flour, shaking off and reserving any excess. Heat the butter in a large frying pan and brown the chops quickly on both sides. Remove the chops from the pan and set aside, then cook the kidneys until browned. Layer half the potato slices in the base of the casserole, then top with the chops and the kidneys.

2. ~Add the onion and carrot to the frying pan and cook until the carrot begins to brown. Layer on top of the chops and kidneys. Sprinkle the reserved flour over the base of the pan and cook, stirring, until dark brown. Gradually pour in the stock and bring to the boil, stirring. Season well with salt and cracked black pepper, and add the thyme and bay leaf. Reduce the heat and simmer for 10 minutes, then pour the mixture into the casserole.

3. ~Layer the remaining potato over the top, covering the meat and vegetables. Cover and cook in the oven for 1 1/4 hours. Remove the lid, brush the potato with butter and cook for a further 30 minutes, or until the potato is brown.

**NUTRITION PER SERVE**
Protein 20 g; Fat 11 g; Carbohydrate 8 g; Dietary Fibre 1.5 g; Cholesterol 150 mg; 890 kJ (212 cal)

**Note** ~Keeps well in the refrigerator for up to 3 days.

*Cut the kidneys in half and remove the cores, then cut into quarters.*

*Layer the onion and carrot over the chops and kidneys.*

*Cook the flour until it turns dark brown, then gradually pour in the stock.*

*Cover the meat and vegetables with the remaining slices of potato.*

# ～ Italian Meatballs ～

**Preparation time:**
50 minutes
**Total cooking time:**
1 hour 30 minutes
**Serves 4**

*Tomato Sauce*
**2 tablespoons olive oil**
**2 cloves garlic, finely
chopped**
**1 red onion, finely
chopped**
**2 x 400 g cans chopped
tomatoes**
**1 cup (250 ml) white
wine**
**1 tablespoon tomato
paste**
**1 teaspoon caster
sugar**
**1 tablespoon chopped
fresh basil**
**1 tablespoon chopped
fresh parsley**
**5 cm strip lemon rind**

*Meatballs*
**3 slices white bread,
crusts removed,
cubed**
**1/3 cup (80 ml) milk**
**500 g veal mince**
**2 cloves garlic, crushed**
**1 small onion, finely
chopped**
**1/4 cup (15 g) chopped
fresh parsley**
**2 teaspoons grated
lemon rind**
**1 egg, lightly beaten**
**1/4 cup (25 g) grated
Parmesan**
**1/2 teaspoon nutmeg**
**flour, for coating**
**oil, for shallow-frying**
**finely chopped fresh
parsley, to garnish**
**grated Parmesan,
to serve**

**1.** ～To make the tomato sauce, heat the olive oil in a 2.5 litre flameproof casserole. Add the garlic and onion and cook for 2–3 minutes, or until softened. Add the tomato, white wine, tomato paste, sugar, basil, parsley, lemon rind and 1/2 cup (125 ml) water. Simmer for 45 minutes, stirring frequently. Remove the lemon rind from the casserole.

**2.** ～To make the meatballs, soak the bread in a small bowl of milk. Leave for 5 minutes to soften the bread, then squeeze out any excess liquid with your hands. Put the bread in a large mixing bowl with the mince, garlic, onion, parsley, lemon rind, egg, Parmesan and nutmeg. Season well with salt and black pepper. Mix together with your hands until all of the ingredients are thoroughly combined.

**3.** ～Form 2 tablespoons of the mixture into balls using wet hands (you will have about 16 balls). Roll the meatballs lightly in the plain flour to coat. Place 1 cm depth of oil in a large heavy-based frying pan over moderate heat. Cook the meatballs in batches for 2–3 minutes on all sides, or until golden brown. Add the meatballs to the tomato sauce and stir to coat. Simmer, covered, over low heat for 30 minutes.

Sprinkle on the parsley and serve with pasta. Top with freshly grated Parmesan.

**NUTRITION PER SERVE**
Protein 17 g; Fat 27 g; Carbohydrate 4.5 g; Dietary Fibre 15 g; Cholesterol 60 mg; 2145 kJ (510 cal)

**Note** ～This casserole will keep in an airtight container in the refrigerator for up to 3 days. Make sure the meatballs are heated through completely before serving.

Soak the bread in milk for 5 minutes, then squeeze out the liquid with your hands.

With clean, wet hands form the mixture into balls and lightly coat in flour.

# ～ Cioppino ～

**Preparation time:**
40 minutes +
30 minutes soaking
**Total cooking time:**
1 hour
**Serves 4**

| | |
|---|---|
| 2 dried porcini mushrooms | 2–3 cloves garlic, crushed |
| 1 kg firm white fish fillets | 1 cup (250 ml) tomato juice |
| 375 g raw king prawns | 425 g can crushed tomatoes |
| 1 raw lobster tail | 1 cup (250 ml) white wine |
| 12 mussels | 1 cup (250 ml) fish stock |
| 1/4 cup (60 ml) olive oil | 6 fresh basil leaves, chopped |
| 1 large onion, finely chopped | 1 bay leaf |
| 1 green capsicum, finely chopped | 2 sprigs fresh parsley |

**1** ～ Soak the dried mushrooms for 20 minutes, then drain, squeeze dry and chop finely. Cut the fish into bite-size pieces, and remove any bones. Peel and devein the prawns, leaving the tails intact. Remove the meat from the lobster shell and cut into small pieces. Discard any open mussels that do not close when tapped; scrub the rest and remove the beards.
**2** ～ Heat the oil in a 2.5 litre flameproof casserole. Cook the onion, capsicum and garlic over medium heat for about 5 minutes, or until the onion is soft. Add the mushrooms, tomato juice, tomatoes, wine, stock and basil. Tie the bay leaf and parsley together with string and add to the casserole. Bring to the boil, then reduce the heat, cover and simmer for 30 minutes.
**3** ～ Add the fish and prawns to the casserole and mix gently. Cook, covered, over low heat for 10 minutes, or until the prawns are pink and the fish is cooked. Add the lobster and mussels and simmer for 2–3 minutes, or until heated through. Discard any unopened mussels and remove the bay leaf. Season to taste with salt and cracked pepper, and serve with crusty bread.

**NUTRITION PER SERVE**
Protein 70 g; Fat 25 g; Carbohydrate 7.75 g; Dietary Fibre 3 g; Cholesterol 325 mg; 660 kJ (155 cal)

*With clean hands, peel and devein the prawns, leaving the tails intact.*

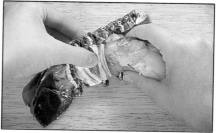

*Cut through the lobster shell on each side of the tail, pull it back and remove the meat.*

*Scrub the mussels thoroughly, then remove their beards.*

*Tie the bay leaf and parsley together with kitchen string.*

# ～ Pot au Feu ～

**Preparation time:**
45 minutes
**Total cooking time:**
2 hours 50 minutes
**Serves 8–10**

1 small veal knuckle
1.3 kg piece gravy beef
bouquet garni
1 kg (size 10) whole
  chicken
4 carrots, halved
8 small onions, studded
  with 2 whole cloves
  each

2 leeks, trimmed, each
  cut into 8 pieces
4 turnips, peeled and
  halved
2 celery sticks, each
  cut into 4 pieces
1 chorizo or large
  Italian sausage
chopped fresh parsley,
  to garnish

**1** ～ Place the veal bone in the base of a 6.5 litre stock pot. Place the gravy beef piece on top, add the bouquet garni and cover with water. Bring rapidly to the boil, skimming off the scum with a large spoon as it rises to the surface.
**2** ～ As soon as the water boils, reduce the heat to a very low simmer, and cover the pot with the lid slightly ajar. Simmer for 1 hour. Skim regularly and top with a little cold water to keep the meat covered.
**3** ～ To truss the chicken, place a length of kitchen string under the parsons nose and up and over the legs, under the wings, then wrap back around the wings. Turn the chicken over onto its breast to cross the string over the back of the chicken. Turn the chicken back over again and tie the legs together.
**4** ～ Add the chicken to the casserole and cook

for a further 30 minutes at a low simmer. Keep covered with the water. Add the carrots, onions, leeks, turnips, celery and chorizo or sausage. Cook for a further 40–50 minutes, or until the chicken and vegetables are tender. Remove the bouquet garni. Arrange the meats and vegetables on a large serving platter, cover with foil and keep warm in the oven.
**5** ～ Strain the broth through a muslin-lined sieve into a large pan. Bring slowly to the boil, then boil for about 15 minutes to reduce the broth by about a quarter and to concentrate the flavours. Reserve about 2 cups (500 ml) of the broth and ladle the rest into a serving jug.
**6** ～ Pot au Feu is served

in two courses. As a first course, ladle the broth into individual soup bowls and serve hot. For the second course, carve the meats at the table and serve with the vegetables. Moisten the meats with the reserved broth. Traditionally served with shredded boiled cabbage, boiled potatoes, French mustard and gherkins. Garnish with parsley.

**NUTRITION PER SERVE (10)**
Protein 55 g; Fat 25 g;
Carbohydrate 30 g; Dietary
Fibre 10 g; Cholesterol 35 mg;
3100 kJ (740 cal)

**Note** ～ This dish can be stored in a large airtight container in the refrigerator for up to 3 days. Freeze any leftover broth as it can be used as a stock base for other soups or casseroles.

*Place the string up and over the legs, under the wings and wrap back around the wings.*

*Turn the chicken onto its breast and cross the string over the back of the chicken.*

# ～ Chicken à la King ～

**Preparation time:**
30 minutes
**Total cooking time:**
1 hour
**Serves 4–6**

*Velouté Sauce*
**50 g butter**
**1/3 cup (40 g) plain
flour**
**2 1/2 cups (600 ml)
chicken stock**
**quarter of an onion,
studded with 3 whole
cloves**
**2 bay leaves**
**1 tablespoon sherry**

**50 g butter**
**1 kg chicken breast
fillets, cut into bite-
size cubes**
**1 onion, chopped**
**125 g button
mushrooms, sliced**
**1 green capsicum,
seeded and cut into
3 cm cubes**
**1 red capsicum, seeded
and cut into 3 cm cubes**
**1/2 cup (125 ml) cream**
**1/3 cup (20 g) chopped
fresh parsley**

**1** ～ To make the velouté sauce, heat the butter in a heavy-based pan. Add the flour and cook over low heat for 2–3 minutes, or until it turns a light nut brown colour. Gradually add the chicken stock, stirring until smooth and thickened. Add the onion piece studded with cloves to the pan with the bay leaves. Cook for 5 minutes, then remove the onion, and bay leaf. Stir in the sherry, then cover the surface with plastic wrap and set aside.
**2** ～ Melt the butter in a large flameproof casserole. Cook the chicken in batches over high heat for 2 minutes, or until well browned. Remove. Add the onion and mushrooms to the casserole, and cook, stirring, for 2 minutes, then add the capsicum and cook for a further 5 minutes.
**3** ～ Return the chicken pieces to the casserole and pour on the velouté sauce. Stir to combine. Cook, covered, over low heat for 30 minutes, stirring two or three times during cooking. Stir in the cream and parsley, season well with salt and cracked pepper and serve with steamed rice.

**NUTRITION PER SERVE (6)**
Protein 40 g; Fat 27 g;
Carbohydrate 8.5 g; Dietary
Fibre 1.7 g; Cholesterol
150 mg; 1838 kJ (440 cal)

*Cook the butter and flour over low heat until it turns a light nut brown.*

*Once the sauce has thickened, remove the onion and bay leaf.*

# ～ Beef Olives ～

**Preparation time:**
1 hour
**Total cooking time:**
1 hour 25 minutes
**Serves 4**

*Stuffing*
2 cups (160 g) fresh
white breadcrumbs
1/3 cup (20 g) chopped
fresh parsley
1/2 teaspoon grated
lemon rind
pinch nutmeg
1 egg, lightly beaten
1 tablespoon dry white
wine

4 slices skirt steak, halved
50 g butter

*Sauce*
185 g mushrooms
2 cloves garlic, crushed
1 red onion, chopped
2 cups (500 ml) beef stock
1 tablespoon plain flour
20 g butter
1/4 cup (15 g) finely
chopped fresh parsley

1.～Preheat the oven to warm 160°C (315°F/ Gas 2–3). Put the breadcrumbs, parsley, lemon rind and nutmeg in a bowl. Mix in the egg and wine with a fork. Season well.
2.～Lay each piece of meat between two sheets of plastic wrap and pound with a rolling pin to about 16 x 14 cm. Divide the stuffing among the meat pieces, shape into a sausage, then roll the meat into a parcel. Tuck in the ends and tie with string. Repeat with the remaining meat.
3.～Heat the butter in a 2.5 litre flameproof casserole. Brown the beef

parcels for 2–3 minutes. Remove. Finely chop the mushrooms and add to the casserole with the garlic and onion. Cook, stirring, for 5 minutes, or until softened. Add the stock and stir for 1–2 minutes. Arrange the beef olives in the casserole in a single layer. Bake for 1 hour, or until tender.
4.～Remove the string from the beef. Cover and set aside. Combine the flour and butter in a

bowl to form a paste. Return the casserole to the stove top and gradually whisk in the paste. Stir until the sauce boils and thickens. Return the beef olives to the casserole and reheat gently on the stove top. Cut the beef olives into 3–4 slices and top with the sauce and parsley.

**NUTRITION PER SERVE**
Protein 30 g; Fat 20 g; Carbohydrate 30 g; Dietary Fibre 3 g; Cholesterol 155 mg; 1785 kJ (425 cal)

*Mix in the egg and wine with a fork until well combined.*

*Lay the meat between two sheets of plastic wrap and gently pound with a rolling pin.*

*Shape the filling like a sausage along the meat, then wrap and roll into a neat parcel.*

*Cook and turn the parcels until they are well browned.*

# ~ Osso Buco with Gremolata ~

**Preparation time:**
40 minutes
**Total cooking time:**
2 hours 20 minutes
**Serves 4**

*Gremolata*
**1 tablespoon finely
zested or grated
lemon rind
1–2 cloves garlic,
finely chopped
1/4 cup (7 g) finely
chopped flat-leaf
parsley**

*Osso Buco*
**4 veal shank pieces,
each 4 cm thick
1/4 cup (30 g) plain
flour**

**2 tablespoons olive oil
2 large onions, sliced
1 carrot, diced
1 celery stick, diced
2–3 cloves garlic,
crushed
6 Roma tomatoes,
finely chopped
2 tablespoons tomato
paste
11/2 cups (375 ml) dry
white wine
1 cup (30 g) finely
chopped flat-leaf
parsley**

**1**.~To make the gremolata, combine the lemon rind, garlic and parsley in a bowl.
**2**.~Coat the veal with seasoned flour, and shake off any excess. Heat half the oil in a 2.5 litre flameproof casserole large enough to fit the meat in a single layer, then brown the veal well on all sides. Remove and set aside.
**3**.~Heat the remaining oil in the casserole and cook the onion, carrot, celery and garlic for 5 minutes, or until soft but not brown. Add the meat in a single layer, to sit snugly in the casserole. Season well.

**4**.~Mix together the tomato, tomato paste and white wine and pour over the meat. Bring to the boil, then reduce the heat, cover and simmer for 1 1/2 hours.
**5**.~Add the parsley to the casserole. Simmer, uncovered, for about 30 minutes, or until the meat is very tender and the sauce has thickened. If you wish to reduce the

sauce further, remove the meat and boil the sauce briskly. This dish is traditionally served with saffron-flavoured risotto (better known as Risotto alla Milanese). Sprinkle the gremolata over the top.

**NUTRITION PER SERVE**
Protein 30 g; Fat 35 g;
Carbohydrate 30 g; Dietary
Fibre 5 g; Cholesterol 114 mg;
2580 kJ (615 cal)

*Combine the lemon rind, garlic and parsley to make the gremolata.*

*Add the veal to the casserole and brown very well on all sides.*

# ~ Pork Braised in Red Cabbage ~

**Preparation time:**
30 minutes
**Total cooking time:**
4 hours 20 minutes
**Serves 4–6**

30 g butter
1 large onion, chopped
1 carrot, diced
140 g bacon, rind
  removed, cut into thin
  strips
1 kg red cabbage, outer
  leaves removed
2 green apples, peeled,
  cored and chopped
2 garlic cloves, crushed
¼ teaspoon ground
  nutmeg

¼ teaspoon ground
  cloves
1½ cups (375 ml) red
  wine
1½ cups (375 ml) beef
  stock
1.5 kg pork neck,
  trimmed of fat
20 g butter, extra
¼ cup (15 g) chopped
  fresh parsley

**1.** Preheat the oven to slow 150°C (300°F/ Gas 2). Heat the butter in a 2.5 litre flameproof casserole. Cook the onion, carrot and bacon, covered, over low heat for 10 minutes. Cut the cabbage into shreds. Stir into the onion mixture, and cook, covered, for a further 10 minutes.

**2.** Add the apple, garlic, nutmeg and cloves. Stir in the red wine and stock, bring to the boil and season well. Cover and cook in the oven for 2 hours.

**3.** Meanwhile, tie the pork neck with kitchen string to keep in shape.

Heat the extra butter in a large frying pan. Add the pork neck and brown evenly all over. Put the meat on top of the cabbage, cover and bake a further 2 hours.

**4.** To serve, remove the string from the pork and transfer to a serving platter. Use a slotted spoon to arrange the cabbage around the pork. Sprinkle with the chopped parsley before serving.

NUTRITION PER SERVE (6)
Protein 55 g; Fat 12 g;
Carbohydrate 15 g; Dietary
Fibre 10 g; Cholesterol
135 mg; 1855 kJ (445 cal)

**Note.** This is not suitable for freezing, but can be stored in an airtight container in the refrigerator for up to 2 days.

**Hint.** Use stainless steel equipment as red cabbage can react to some metals and turn a blueish colour.

*Cut the cabbage into shreds and stir into the onion mixture.*

*Tie the pork neck with kitchen string to keep it in shape during cooking.*

# ~ Chicken Tagine ~

**Preparation time:**
25 minutes + 2 hours
chilling
**Total cooking time:**
2 hours 15 minutes
**Serves 4**

2 cloves garlic,
  chopped
1 teaspoon ground
  ginger
1/4 teaspoon saffron
  threads or powder
1 teaspoon hot paprika
1/2 teaspoon ground
  cumin
1 kg chicken pieces
1 tablespoon oil

1 large onion,
  chopped
1/4 cup (7 g) fresh
  coriander leaves,
  finely chopped
2 cups (500 ml) chicken
  stock or water
250 g pitted prunes
1 tablespoon honey
1 teaspoon grated
  orange rind
1 cinnamon stick

1. Combine the garlic, ginger, saffron, paprika, cumin and 1/2 teaspoon black pepper in a bowl. Toss the chicken pieces in the spices, then cover and refrigerate for 2 hours.
2. Heat the oil in a 2.5 litre flameproof casserole and lightly brown the chicken in batches.
3. Add the onion and coriander. Mix well, then pour on enough stock or water to cover. Simmer, covered, over low heat for 1 1/2 hours.
4. Add the prunes, honey, orange rind and cinnamon stick, then

cook, uncovered, for 25 minutes, or until the sauce has reduced a little. Remove the cinnamon stick before serving on a bed of couscous, garnished with toasted slivered almonds.

**NUTRITION PER SERVE**
Protein 60 g; Fat 10 g; Carbohydrate 35 g; Dietary Fibre 5.5 g; Cholesterol 125 mg; 1975 kJ (470 cal)

**Note** Tagines take their names from the

shallow earthenware pots with conical lids in which they are cooked. They are North African in origin.
**Variation** Replace the prunes with an equal quantity of fresh quince pieces or dried fruits such as apricots or dates.
**Hint** Paprika comes in more than one variety. For this recipe, make sure you buy the hot paprika, not the sweet paprika.

*Use a sharp knife to finely chop the fresh coriander leaves.*

*Add the chicken pieces to the bowl and toss in the spices.*

*Stir in the onion and coriander, then cover the chicken pieces with stock or water.*

*Add the prunes, honey, orange rind and cinnamon stick to the casserole.*

# ~ Carbonade à la Flamande ~

**Preparation time:**
30 minutes
**Total cooking time:**
1 hour 45 minutes
**Serves 4–6**

1.25 kg gravy beef,
  trimmed and cut into
  4 cm cubes
30 g butter
1 tablespoon oil
20 g butter, extra
2 large onions, sliced
  into rings
3 cloves garlic, chopped
1 tablespoon plain flour

1¹/₂ cups (375 ml)
  brown ale or stout
1 tablespoon tomato
  paste
1 tablespoon soft brown
  sugar
bouquet garni
fresh thyme leaves,
  to garnish

1 ~ Preheat the oven to moderate 180°C (350°F/Gas 4). Pat the beef cubes dry with paper towels. Heat half the butter and oil in a 2.5 litre flameproof casserole, and cook half the beef over high heat for 2–3 minutes, or until browned all over. Remove to a side plate. Heat the remaining butter and oil and brown the remaining beef, then remove to the side plate.
2 ~ Heat the extra butter in the casserole, and cook the onion and garlic for 2–3 minutes. Stir in the flour and cook for 1 minute. Add the beer, tomato paste and brown sugar, and stir to lift any bits that may be stuck to the bottom of the casserole. Cook, stirring, until the sauce boils and thickens.
3 ~ Return the beef to the casserole and add the bouquet garni. Put the casserole in the oven and cook, covered, for 1¹/₂ hours, or until the beef is tender. Remove the bouquet garni and skim off any fat from the surface. Season well with salt and cracked black pepper and garnish with fresh thyme leaves. This dish is delicious served with mashed potato, and is often garnished with slices of bread, spread with mustard and grilled.

**NUTRITION PER SERVE (6)**
Protein 45 g; Fat 15 g; Carbohydrate 9 g; Dietary Fibre 1 g; Cholesterol 160 mg; 1605 kJ (385 cal)

**Note** ~ This classic Flemish dish originated in Belgium and gets its characteristic flavour and colour from brown ale or stout.

*Stir the flour through the onion mixture before pouring in the beer.*

*Return the beef to the casserole and add the bouquet garni.*

# ～ Rabbit Casserole with Mustard Sauce ～

**Preparation time:**
30 minutes
**Total cooking time:**
2 hours
**Serves 4**

2 rabbits (800 g each)
2 tablespoons vegetable
    oil
2 onions, sliced
4 rashers bacon, cut
    into 3 cm pieces
2 tablespoons plain
    flour
1¹/2 cups (375 ml)
    chicken stock or water
¹/2 cup (125 ml) white
    wine
sprig fresh thyme
¹/2 cup (125 ml) cream
2 tablespoons Dijon
    mustard
fresh thyme sprigs,
    to garnish

1.～Preheat the oven to moderate 180°C (350°F/Gas 4). Remove any fat from the rabbit and wash under running cold water. Pat dry with paper towels. Cut along both sides of the backbone with kitchen scissors and discard, then cut the rabbit into eight even-sized pieces and pat dry again.

2.～Heat half the oil in a 2.5 litre flameproof casserole. Brown half the rabbit, then remove. Add the remaining oil, brown the remaining rabbit, and remove.

3.～Add the onion and bacon to the casserole, and cook, stirring, for 3 minutes, or until lightly browned. Sprinkle on the flour and mix well. Stir with a wooden spoon to lift the baked-on sediment from the side of the pan— this gives colour to the sauce. Add the stock or water and wine, and stir until the sauce boils and thickens. Return the rabbit to the pan.

Add the thyme sprig.
4.～Cover and bake for 1¹/4–1¹/2 hours, or until the rabbit is tender and the sauce has thickened. Remove the sprig of thyme, and stir through the combined cream and mustard. Garnish with thyme sprigs and serve with steamed potatoes.

**NUTRITION PER SERVE**
Protein 50 g; Fat 20 g; Carbohydrate 10 g; Dietary Fibre 1 g; Cholesterol 150 mg; 1670 kJ (835 cal)

*Using kitchen scissors, cut along either side of the backbone and discard.*

*Cut the rabbit into eight even-sized pieces, then pat dry again.*

*Heat the oil in the casserole and brown the rabbit pieces in two batches.*

*Return the rabbit pieces to the casserole, then add the thyme sprig.*

# ～ Veal Marengo ～

**Preparation time:**
40 minutes
**Total cooking time:**
2 hours 40 minutes
**Serves 4**

1 kg leg or shoulder
  veal, cubed
1 tablespoon olive oil
20 g butter
2 large onions, chopped
2 cloves garlic, chopped
1 tablespoon plain flour
1 1/2 cups (375 ml) white
  wine
500 g tomatoes, peeled,
  seeded and chopped
2 tablespoons tomato
  paste

5 cm piece orange rind
2 teaspoons chopped
  fresh thyme
30 g butter, extra
185 g mushrooms,
  sliced
2 teaspoons cornflour
1 tablespoon white
  wine, extra
fresh thyme, to garnish
oil, for shallow-frying
3 slices white bread,
  crusts removed

1.～Preheat the oven to warm 160°C (315°F/ Gas 2–3). Pat the veal dry with paper towels. Heat half the oil in a 2.5 litre flameproof casserole. Brown half the veal over high heat, then repeat with the remaining oil and veal.
2.～Heat the butter in the casserole and cook the onion and garlic for 2–3 minutes. Stir in the flour. Cook for 1 minute. Add the wine, and stir to lift the sediment from the base of the casserole. Cook, stirring, until the mixture boils and thickens slightly. Add the tomato, tomato paste, rind and thyme.

3.～Return the veal to the casserole, then cook, covered, in the oven for 1 1/2 hours. Heat the extra butter in a frying pan, cook the mushrooms and add to the casserole. Cook for 15 minutes, or until the veal is tender. Remove the orange rind.
4.～Return the casserole to the stove top and stir in the combined cornflour and wine until thickened. Garnish with the fresh thyme sprigs.

5.～Heat enough oil in a pan to 1 cm depth. Cut the bread into triangles and fry on both sides in the hot oil in batches until golden brown, adding more oil as necessary. Drain well on paper towels, and serve immediately with the veal.

**NUTRITION PER SERVE**
Protein 60 g; Fat 35 g; Carbohydrate 18 g; Dietary Fibre 4 g; Cholesterol 235 mg; 3000 kJ (717 cal)

*Pour in the white wine and stir to lift the sediment from the base of the casserole.*

*Return the veal to the casserole with the tomato, tomato paste, rind and thyme.*

*Fry the mushrooms in butter, then add them to the casserole.*

*Heat the oil, then cook the bread triangles in batches.*

# ～ Coq au Vin ～

**Preparation time:**
40 minutes
**Total cooking time:**
1 hour 30 minutes
**Serves 6**

30 g butter
1 tablespoon oil
12 pickling onions
3 bacon rashers,
   rind removed,
   chopped
12 button mushrooms
1 carrot, sliced
1 onion, sliced
2 kg chicken pieces

2 tablespoons brandy
2 cups (500 ml) dry
   red wine
3/4 cup (185 ml) chicken
   stock
1 bouquet garni
2 tablespoons flour
2 tablespoons butter,
   extra

**1** ～ Heat half the butter and oil in a 2.5 litre flameproof casserole and cook the pickling onions for 5–8 minutes, or until brown. Remove from the casserole and set aside. Add the bacon and mushrooms, and fry until the bacon is browned, then remove.
**2** ～ Heat the remaining butter and oil in the casserole, add the carrot and onion, and cook until browned. Remove. Add the chicken pieces and fry for 5 minutes, or until golden all over. Remove the casserole from the heat and stir in the brandy. Add the wine, stock, bouquet garni and carrot and onion mixture. Return to the heat and bring the mixture to the boil, then reduce the heat, cover and simmer for 40–50 minutes, or until the chicken is tender. Remove the chicken pieces, strain the sauce into a bowl and discard the carrot, onion and bouquet garni.
**3** ～ Combine the flour and butter to form a paste. Return the sauce to the casserole and gradually whisk in the paste and stir until the sauce boils and thickens.

Return the chicken, pickling onions, mushrooms and bacon to the casserole. Simmer for 5–10 minutes, or until heated through. Serve with crusty French bread.

**NUTRITION PER SERVE**
Protein 80 g; Fat 20 g;
Carbohydrate 8 g; Dietary
Fibre 2 g; Cholesterol
205 mg; 2591 kJ (619 cal)

**Note** ～ As with any recipe it is always worth cooking with a wine you would drink. Try a nice Cabernet Sauvignon or Merlot for this recipe.

*Cook the pickling onions in the butter and oil until brown.*

*Fry the mushrooms and bacon together in the casserole.*

*Add the wine, stock, bouquet garni and carrot and onion mixture.*

*Gradually whisk the flour and butter paste into the sauce.*

# ∼ Pork with Prunes ∼

**Preparation time:**
25 minutes +
30 minutes soaking
**Total cooking time:**
1 hour 25 minutes
**Serves 4–6**

20 (165 g) large pitted
    prunes
10 blanched almonds
2 large pork fillets, cut
    in half (about 1 kg)
20 g butter
1 tablespoon oil
1 tablespoon plain flour
1 cup (250 ml) beef stock
1 tablespoon
    redcurrant jelly
2/3 cup (170 ml) white
    wine
12 French shallots,
    peeled and halved
    (if large)
1/4 cup (60 ml) cream

**1**∼Soak the prunes in water or cold tea for 30 minutes to plump, then drain well. Stuff 10 of the prunes with an almond and reserve the remaining prunes.
**2**∼Make a slit down the centre of each pork fillet, open it out and fill with the stuffed prunes. Enclose and tie securely with string.
**3**∼Heat the butter and oil in a large frying pan and brown the pork fillets evenly all over. Transfer to a 2.5 litre flameproof casserole and arrange the fillets in a single layer. Sprinkle the flour onto the fat in the frying pan and stir to combine. Gradually stir in the stock, then the jelly and half of the white wine. Cook, stirring, until the sauce boils and thickens, then pour over the pork fillets. Simmer, covered, over very low heat for 40 minutes, or until the pork is tender.
**4**∼Put the remaining prunes in a pan with the remaining wine. Simmer for 10 minutes, or until the wine has evaporated. Put the shallots in a pan and cover with water, bring to the boil and cook for 10 minutes, or until tender. Drain.
**5**∼To serve, remove the string from the pork. Cut into thick slices and arrange on a serving platter. Add the reserved prunes, shallots and cream to the sauce, and reheat without boiling. Coat the pork with some of the sauce and arrange the prunes and shallots around the pork slices.

**NUTRITION PER SERVE (6)**
Protein 40 g; Fat 15 g; Carbohydrate 15 g; Dietary Fibre 2.5 g; Cholesterol 105 mg; 1555 kJ (370 cal)

*Make a slit down the centre of each fillet, open it out and put the prunes in the centre.*

*Tie the fillets securely with kitchen string and brown them evenly all over.*

*Whisk the beef stock into the pan, then add the jelly and half the wine.*

*Add the prunes, shallots and cream to the sauce and gently reheat.*

# ～ Estouffade of Beef ～

**Preparation time:**
40 minutes
**Total cooking time:**
2 hours 25 minutes
**Serves 4**

1 kg beef (chuck, skirt or round), trimmed
1/4 cup (30 g) plain flour
20 g butter
2 tablespoons olive oil
4 rashers bacon, rind removed, diced
3 onions, each cut into 8 wedges
2 cups (500 ml) dry red wine
1 sprig thyme
2 bay leaves
2 cloves garlic, chopped
30 g butter, extra
250 g mushrooms, sliced
1/3 cup (20 g) finely chopped fresh parsley

1.～Preheat the oven to warm 160°C (315°F/ Gas 2–3). Cut the beef into 4 cm cubes, then coat in the flour in batches. Shake off and reserve any excess flour. Heat the butter and half the oil in a 2.5 litre flameproof casserole. Cook the meat over high heat for 2–3 minutes, or until well browned. Cook in batches, adding extra oil if necessary.

2.～ Heat the remaining oil in a large frying pan. Add the bacon and onion and cook, stirring, for 3–4 minutes, or until softened. Add to the meat in the casserole and stir to combine.

3.～Sprinkle the reserved flour into the frying pan and pour in the red wine. Stir to dissolve any sediment, bring to the boil then pour over the meat. Tie the thyme sprig to the bay leaves with kitchen string and add to the casserole with the garlic. Cook, covered, in the oven for 2 hours, or until the meat is tender.

4.～Meanwhile, heat the extra butter in a pan, add the mushrooms and cook for 2–3 minutes, then set aside.

5.～Remove the meat from the sauce with a slotted spoon and set aside. Place the casserole over high heat and boil the sauce until reduced by about a third. Remove the bay leaves and thyme and add the mushrooms. Return the meat to the casserole and simmer gently for 10 minutes. Sprinkle on the parsley and serve.

**NUTRITION PER SERVE**
Protein 65 g; Fat 30 g; Carbohydrate 10 g; Dietary Fibre 3.5 g; Cholesterol 220 mg; 2672 kJ (660 cal)

*Place the beef cubes in a plastic bag with the flour and shake to coat.*

*Pour the red wine into the pan and stir with a wooden spoon to dissolve any sediment.*

*Tie the thyme sprig and bay leaves together with kitchen string.*

*Remove the meat from the sauce with a slotted spoon.*

# ~ Irish Stew ~

**Preparation time:**
20 minutes
**Total cooking time:**
1 hour 15 minutes
**Serves 4**

---

8 lamb neck chops
30 g butter
1 kg potatoes, thickly
 sliced
3 onions, sliced into
 thick rounds

3 carrots, sliced
2 cups (500 ml) beef or
 vegetable stock
sprigs of fresh thyme,
 to taste

---

**1.** ~ Trim the chops of excess fat. Melt the butter in a 2.5 litre flameproof casserole and brown the chops in batches on both sides over high heat. Remove and drain well.
**2.** ~ Arrange half the potato, onion and carrot in the casserole and season with salt and pepper. Layer the chops on top and cover with the remaining potato, onion and carrot. Add the stock and thyme.
**3.** ~ Cover and bring to the boil, then reduce the heat and simmer for about 1 hour, or until the lamb is tender.

**NUTRITION PER SERVE**
Protein 40 g; Fat 15 g; Carbohydrate 40 g; Dietary Fibre 7 g; Cholesterol 115 mg; 1930 kJ (460 cal)

**Note** ~ Irish stew is traditionally made from mutton, without potatoes or carrots. Adding vegetables makes a satisfying one-pot meal.

*Use a sharp knife to trim the chops of excess fat.*

*Brown the chops on both sides and drain on paper towels.*

*Layer half the potato, onion and carrot over the bottom of the casserole.*

*Top with the remaining vegetables and pour in the stock.*

# ~ Chicken Paprika ~

**Preparation time:**
30 minutes
**Total cooking time:**
1 hour 20 minutes
**Serves 4–6**

1.5 kg chicken pieces
30 g butter
1 tablespoon olive oil
2 onions, thinly sliced
2 tablespoons
  Hungarian paprika
1 tablespoon plain flour
400 g can tomatoes,
  roughly chopped
1 cup (250 g) sour
  cream
1 tablespoon lemon
  juice
1/3 cup (20 g) chopped
  fresh parsley

1. ~ Preheat the oven to moderate 180°C (350°F/Gas 4). Remove any excess fat and skin from the chicken pieces and pat dry with paper towels. Season well with cracked black pepper. Heat the butter and oil in a 2.5 litre flameproof casserole. Add half of the chicken pieces and cook, turning, for 3–4 minutes, or until golden brown. Remove to a side plate, then repeat with the remaining chicken pieces.

2. ~ Add the onion to the casserole and cook for 2–3 minutes, or until softened. Add the paprika and cook for a further 1 minute. Stir in the flour, cook for 1 minute more, then stir in the tomatoes and 1/2 cup (125 ml) water. Stir over medium heat until the sauce boils and thickens, then reduce the heat and simmer for 2 minutes.

3. ~ Return the chicken to the casserole and coat well with the sauce. Cover and place in the oven, and cook for 1 hour, or until the chicken pieces are tender. Remove the chicken from the casserole and arrange on a warmed serving plate.

4. ~ Stir the sour cream through the sauce and reheat without allowing to boil. Add lemon juice to taste and season well with salt. Spoon the sauce over the chicken, sprinkle with parsley and serve with pasta.

NUTRITION PER SERVE (6)
Protein 60 g; Fat 30 g; Carbohydrate 6.5 g; Dietary Fibre 1.5 g; Cholesterol 190 mg; 2220 kJ (530 cal)

**Note** ~ Good-quality fresh paprika is essential to make this dish a success. It should be fragrant with a dark reddish pink colour.

*Use a sharp knife to remove excess fat and skin from the chicken.*

*Cook the onion until softened, then add the paprika.*

*Add the tomato and water and stir until the sauce is thickened and smooth.*

*Put the chicken pieces back into the casserole and cover with the sauce.*

# ～ Steak and Kidney Hotpot with Herb Dumplings ～

**Preparation time:**
30 minutes
**Total cooking time:**
2 hours 30 minutes
**Serves 4**

1 tablespoon oil
20 g butter
1 kg round, rump or
skirt steak, cut into
3 cm cubes
250 g lamb kidneys,
cores removed
1 onion, chopped
185 g field mushrooms,
sliced
1/4 cup (30 g) plain flour
1 cup (250 ml) beef
stock

2 teaspoons
Worcestershire sauce

*Herb Dumplings*
1 cup (125 g) plain flour
1 1/2 teaspoons baking
powder
1/4 cup (15 g) chopped
fresh parsley
1 teaspoon chopped
fresh thyme
1 egg, lightly beaten
1/3 cup (80 ml) milk

1.～Preheat the oven to warm 160°C (315°F/Gas 2–3). Heat half the oil and butter in a 2.5 litre flameproof casserole. Brown half the beef and kidneys over high heat for 2 minutes. Remove and repeat with the remaining oil, butter, beef and kidneys.
2.～Add the onion and mushrooms to the casserole. Cook, stirring, for 2 minutes, or until softened. Add the meat and kidneys to the casserole and sprinkle with the flour. Stir to combine for 2 minutes, then pour on the stock and Worcestershire sauce. Cook, stirring, for 2 minutes, or until the sauce boils and thickens. Cook, covered, in the oven for 1 1/2 hours, or until the meat is tender. Add a little more stock or water if you would like to have more sauce.

3.～Increase the oven temperature to moderate 180°C (350°F/Gas 4). Cook the casserole for a further 15–20 minutes while preparing the herb dumplings—the meat juices should be bubbling. Sift the flour, baking powder and 1/2 teaspoon salt into a bowl. Stir through the parsley and thyme, and make a well in the centre. Add the combined egg and milk and use a flat-bladed knife to quickly bring together to a soft dough. Be careful not to overmix. Drop tablespoons of the dough evenly over the casserole. Cover and return to the oven and

cook for 20 minutes without lifting the lid. Remove the lid and cook for a further 5 minutes, or until the dumplings are lightly golden. Serve with mashed potato and steamed vegetables.

**NUTRITION PER SERVE**
Protein 80 g; Fat 20 g; Carbohydrate 32 g; Dietary Fibre 3 g; Cholesterol 440 mg; 2595 kJ (620 cal)

**Note**～This casserole can be prepared and then refrigerated or frozen before adding the dumplings. If frozen, thaw in the refrigerator, add the dumplings and cook as above. Ensure that the casserole is piping hot in the centre before serving.

*Pour in the combined egg and milk and bring together to a soft dough.*

*Drop tablespoons of the dough over the casserole and cook without lifting the lid.*

# ∼ Boston Baked Beans ∼

**Preparation time:**
25 minutes +
overnight soaking
**Total cooking time:**
1 hour 35 minutes
**Serves 4–6**

1³/4 cups (350 g) dried
  cannellini beans
1 whole ham hock
2 onions, chopped
2 tablespoons tomato
  paste
1 tablespoon molasses

1 teaspoon French
  mustard
¹/4 cup (45 g) soft brown
  sugar
¹/2 cup (125 ml) tomato
  juice

1.∼Cover the dried cannellini beans with plenty of cold water and soak overnight.
2.∼Rinse the beans, drain well, then transfer to a 2.5 litre flameproof casserole. Add the ham hock and cover with cold water. Bring to the boil, then reduce the heat and simmer, covered, for 25 minutes, or until the beans are tender. Preheat the oven to warm 160°C (315°F/Gas 2–3).
3.∼Remove the ham hock from the casserole and set aside to cool. Drain the beans, reserving 1 cup (250 ml)
of the cooking liquid. Trim the ham of all skin, fat and sinew. Cut the meat from the bone and roughly chop. Discard the bone.
4.∼Return the meat and beans to the casserole. Add the reserved liquid, onion, tomato paste, molasses, mustard, brown sugar and tomato juice. Mix gently to combine, then cover and bake for 1 hour. Delicious served with hot, buttered toast.

**NUTRITION PER SERVE (6)**
Protein 8 g; Fat 8 g;
Carbohydrate 20 g; Dietary
Fibre 4.5 g; Cholesterol
15 mg; 920 kJ (220 cal)

**Notes**∼Boston baked beans were first created as a weekend ritual during the Puritan era. They were served with brown bread for dinner on Saturday, then served again for breakfast and lunch on Sunday, as cooking was not allowed on the Sabbath.

Any type of dried bean can be used in this recipe. To quick-soak the beans, place them in a pan, add enough hot water to cover, bring slowly to the boil, then remove from the heat. Leave to soak for 1 hour before draining and using.

*Put the cannellini beans in a bowl and cover with cold water.*

*Lift the ham hock out of the casserole with a pair of tongs and set aside to cool.*

*Trim the ham of skin, fat and sinew then cut the meat from the bone.*

*Return the meat and beans to the casserole and add the remaining ingredients.*

# ～ Blanquette de Veau ～

**Preparation time:**
40 minutes
**Total cooking time:**
2 hours
**Serves 4**

1.25 kg leg veal, cut into 5 cm pieces
1 onion, studded with 4 whole cloves
1 large carrot, cut into thirds
1 bouquet garni
12 French shallots or pickling onions, peeled
20 g butter
1 tablespoon lemon juice

185 g small button mushrooms

*Velouté Sauce*
50 g butter
1/4 cup (30 g) plain flour
2 egg yolks
1/2 cup (125 ml) cream
1/3 cup (20 g) chopped fresh parsley

1.～Put the veal pieces in a 2.5 litre flameproof casserole. Add the onion, carrot and bouquet garni, and enough water to cover by 1 cm. Bring to the boil, then simmer, covered, over low heat for 1 1/2 hours. Remove any scum from the top.

2.～Put the shallots or onions in a pan, cover with water, then simmer for 12 minutes, or until tender. Drain. In the same pan, combine the butter, lemon juice and 1 tablespoon of water. Stir in the mushrooms, and cook, covered, for 5 minutes, shaking the pan occasionally. Drain, reserving the liquid.

3.～To make the sauce, remove the meat with a slotted spoon, then strain the liquid, discarding the vegetables and reserving the meat juices. Keep the meat covered and warm. Melt the butter in a pan, add the flour and cook for 1 minute. Gradually add 2 1/3 cups (580 ml) of the meat liquid and all of the mushroom liquid. Stir until the sauce boils and thickens. Simmer for 5 minutes then strain. Return the sauce to

the pan. Whisk in the combined egg yolks and cream without allowing to boil. Add the parsley and season.

4.～Add the onions and mushrooms to the sauce and warm through over low heat. Put the warm veal pieces on a serving dish and spoon over the sauce, mushrooms and onion. Serve with rice.

**NUTRITION PER SERVE**
Protein 72 g; Fat 30 g; Carbohydrate 12 g; Dietary Fibre 3 g; Cholesterol 440 mg; 2598 kJ (620 cal)

*Peel the onion then carefully stud with the cloves.*

*Remove the meat from the casserole with a slotted spoon.*

*Gradually mix the meat and mushroom liquid into the butter and flour roux.*

*Whisk the combined egg yolks and cream into the sauce.*

# ～ Vegetable Tagine ～

**Preparation time:**
20 minutes
**Total cooking time:**
40 minutes
**Serves 4**

| | |
|---|---|
| 1 large potato, chopped | 1 large red chilli, seeded |
| 1 large carrot, chopped | and chopped |
| 1 turnip or swede, | 1 tablespoon ground |
| peeled and chopped | cumin |
| 150 g sweet potato, | 1 cinnamon stick |
| chopped | 1 zucchini, chopped |
| 400 g can tomatoes | 2 baby eggplants, |
| 1¹/2 cups (375 ml) | chopped |
| chicken or vegetable | 100 g blanched almonds |
| stock | 125 g dried apricots |
| 2 tablespoons olive oil | ¹/4 cup (7 g) chopped |
| 2 red onions, chopped | fresh flat-leaf |
| 8 large cloves garlic, | parsley |
| chopped | |

**1** ～ Put the potato, carrot, turnip or swede and sweet potato into a 2.5 litre flameproof casserole. Add the tomatoes and enough chicken or vegetable stock to just cover. Bring slowly to the boil, then reduce the heat, cover and simmer for 15 minutes, or until the vegetables are just tender.

**2** ～ Meanwhile, heat the oil in a frying pan. Cook the onion, garlic and chilli for 5 minutes, or until tender. Add the cumin and cinnamon stick and cook over low heat for a further 3 minutes.

**3** ～ Stir the onion and garlic mixture into the vegetables in the casserole. Add the zucchini, eggplant, almonds and apricots. Stir to combine, then bring slowly to the boil. Simmer, covered, for 10 minutes and then uncovered for a further 5 minutes, or until the vegetables are tender and the liquid has thickened. Stir in the parsley and serve with steamed couscous, harrissa and preserved lemons for a traditional Moroccan dish.

**NUTRITION PER SERVE**
Protein 10 g; Fat 25 g; Carbohydrate 25 g; Dietary Fibre 10 g; Cholesterol 0 mg; 1500 kJ (360 cal)

**Note** ～ For a different flavour, try replacing the parsley with chopped coriander leaves.

*Peel the turnip or swede and chop into large pieces.*

*Put the chopped vegetables into the casserole and add the canned tomatoes.*

*Stir the onion mixture into the vegetables in the casserole.*

*Add the zucchini, eggplant, almonds and apricots and mix well.*

# ～ Chicken Mole ～

**Preparation time:**
1 hour + 35 minutes
soaking
**Total cooking time:**
2 hours 10 minutes
**Serves 4–6**

1.6 kg chicken pieces
6 cloves garlic
2 onions, chopped
50 g mulato chillies
60 g pasilla chillies
60 g ancho chillies
3 whole cloves
3 whole allspice
oil, for cooking
¹/₄ cup (40 g) sesame
seeds

¹/₄ cup (40 g) unsalted
peanuts
8 almonds
2 tablespoons raisins
¹/₂ teaspoon ground
coriander
3 cinnamon sticks,
slivered
90 g Mexican drinking
chocolate or
bittersweet chocolate

**1** Preheat the oven to moderately hot 190°C (375°F/Gas 5). Place the chicken pieces in a 2.5 litre flameproof casserole with 4 cloves of garlic and half the onion. Pour in enough water to cover. Bring to the boil, then reduce the heat and simmer for 30 minutes, or until just tender. Remove the chicken and strain the stock, reserving 1.25 litres.

**2** Cut the chillies open. Remove and reserve the seeds. Bake the chillies for 5 minutes, then put them in a dish, cover with boiling water and soak for 30 minutes.

**3** Cook the chilli seeds in a dry frying pan over medium heat, shaking to brown evenly. Once browned, increase the heat and char until black. Place in a bowl, cover with water and soak for 5 minutes. Drain the seeds and place in a blender or

food processor with the cloves, allspice and ²/₃ cup (170 ml) water.

**4** Heat 1 tablespoon of oil in the casserole. Fry the sesame seeds until dark brown. Add to the blender or food processor, leaving any extra oil in the casserole. Blend well.

**5** Heat another tablespoon of oil. Cook the peanuts, almonds and raisins until the nuts are golden and the raisins puff up, stirring constantly. Place in the blender. Add the coriander and cinnamon and remaining onion and garlic to the pan, cook until golden, then add to the blender. Blend until the mixture is a thick paste, adding a little water if necessary. Heat some oil in the casserole, add the paste and fry for 15 minutes,

scraping the casserole occasionally.

**6** Put half the chillies in the clean blender with ¹/₂ cup (125 ml) of the chilli soaking liquid and blend until smooth, adding more liquid if the mixture becomes too thick. Add the remaining chillies and more liquid and blend until smooth. Add to the casserole with the chocolate, mix well and simmer for 5 minutes. Pour in 1 litre of the stock and stir until well combined. Bring to the boil and simmer for 35 minutes. Add the chicken, season with salt and cook for about 10 minutes. Add a little more stock to thin the sauce if necessary.

**NUTRITION PER SERVE (6)**
Protein 30 g; Fat 15 g;
Carbohydrate 15 g; Dietary
Fibre 3 g; Cholesterol
80 mg; 1265 kJ (305 cal)

*Cut the chillies open and remove the stems, cores and seeds.*

*Add the chilli seeds to a deep frying pan and cook over medium heat.*

# ∿ Index ∿

Front cover: Beef Bourguignon;
Chicken Cacciatore.